Holiday

KING OF THE STABLE

To the other man in my life,
who was also born on Christmas Day.
All my love, Melody

KING OF THE STABLE

Copyright © 1998 by Melody Carlson

Published by Crossway Books
A division of Good News Publishers
1300 Crescent Street,
Wheaton, Illinois 60187

Illustrations by Chris Ellison

Design by Cindy Kiple

First printing, 1998
Printed in the United States of America

LIBRARY OF CONGRESS CATALOGING-IN-PUBLICATION DATA
Carlson, Melody.
King of the stable/by Melody Carlson: [illustrated by Chris Ellison].
p. cm.
Summary: While staying with his uncle, an innkeeper in Bethlehem, Matthew helps
prepare a place for the baby Jesus to be born.
ISBN 1-58134-032-X (alk. paper)
1. Jesus Christ--Nativity--Juvenile fiction. [1. Jesus Christ--Nativity--Fiction.
2. Christmas--Fiction.] I. Ellison, Chris, ill. II. Title.
PZ7.C216637Ki 1998   98-19486
[E]--dc21   CIP
                                                             AC

| 11 | 10 | 09 | 08 | 07 | 06 | 05 | 04 | 03 | 02 | 01 | 00 | 99 | 98 |
| 15 | 14 | 13 | 12 | 11 | 10 | 9 | 8 | 7 | 6 | 5 | 4 | 3 | 2 | 1 |

King
of the
Stable

Melody Carlson

ILLUSTRATED BY

Chris Ellison

CROSSWAY BOOKS · WHEATON, ILLINOIS
A DIVISION OF GOOD NEWS PUBLISHERS

Sometimes life changes in a moment.

One day you're sitting on top of the world,

and the next day you're cleaning out stables.

That's how it was for young Matthew,

and this is his story.

♛

Matthew sensed it the moment he passed through the courtyard. A strange stillness hung over his house like a thick wool blanket. No servants bustled back and forth; no good smells drifted from the cook's quarters. Matthew knew. Something was wrong.

"Father?" he called as he moved through the silent rooms. *Slip-slap, slip-slap*—the soles of his sandals echoed across the cool marble floor. "Father?" he cried, his voice breaking, "where are you?"

It all seemed painfully familiar. On another day their house had been very quiet—just like this. It was the day his mother had died. The servants had crept about in silence, and then the mourners came, filling the halls with their wailing cries. He had never forgotten that sound; he had never wanted to hear it again.

"Father!" he cried desperately. *"Father, where are you?"*

A hand rested upon Matthew's shoulder and he turned to see the kind, wrinkled face of Jacob.

"Your father isn't here," said the gentle old servant.

"Where is he?" asked Matthew. "Is my father all right?"

Jacob nodded. "Your father is fine. But the Romans are keeping him for a while."

Tears filled Matthew's eyes. "When will they let him go?"

"I don't know, Matthew." Jacob shook his head. "But your father asked me to take you to Bethlehem."

"Bethlehem?" Matthew frowned. "What's in Bethlehem?"

"Your mother's brother lives there—your Uncle Isaac. He runs a small inn. You'll stay with him until things are settled with your father. But we must leave at once."

As the two traveled along the dusty road, many questions rumbled through Matthew's mind. He turned to Jacob and asked, "What's my uncle like? What's his home like?"

"He's not rich like your father, and they have no servants," explained Jacob.

"No servants? Then who does the work?"

Old Jacob laughed. "I suppose the whole family pitches in."

Uncle Isaac wrapped thick arms around Matthew and squeezed him tight. "My dear sister's only son," he proclaimed. "I can see you're a fine young man, Matthew."

Matthew was then introduced to Aunt Ruth and his six cousins: Sarah was the oldest, followed by Lydia, Rebecca, Leah, Rachel, and finally Abigail. Matthew frowned at the giggly girls—*not a single boy in the bunch!*

"Your clothes are very pretty," said Rachel as she fingered his fine silk sash.

"You look just like a little king," teased Abigail. The others giggled.

"Hush, girls," said Sarah. "We have lots of guests and lots of work to do."

"Is *he* going to help?" asked Abigail.

"Of course not," mocked Rebecca. "*Little kings* can't work."

"I'm not a king," argued Matthew, "and I *can* work."

Rebecca studied his fancy clothes, then turned to Sarah with a smirk. "He can have my job caring for the animals," she suggested. "Then I can help inside the inn."

Abigail clapped her hands and laughed. "Matthew can be *king of the stable!*"

Rebecca showed Matthew to the stable at the back of the inn. She gave him some quick instructions and told him the names of the livestock before she hurried off.

I'll show those goofy girls that I know how to work, thought Matthew as he stood in the middle of the stable with a pitchfork in hand. *How hard can it be to care for silly old animals anyway?*

Matthew removed his fine tunic and began to work. He shoveled the smelly old straw out and replaced it with fresh. Then he carefully laid sweet-smelling hay in the food mangers and carried water to fill the water troughs. It was hard work, and he could feel blisters burning on his hands. Finally, he paused long enough to stroke Jasmine's velvety nose.

"My life has been turned upside down," Matthew told the cow with a tired sigh. "My father's a wealthy and important man, but here I am cleaning stables like a servant."

Jasmine looked at him with warm, brown eyes and nodded her big head. Matthew frowned, then glanced around the stable at the contented animals. "I guess I *am* the king of the stable."

Throughout the day, Bethlehem was swarmed by travelers until Uncle Isaac's small inn overflowed with guests. All the guests were hungry and tired, and kept Matthew's cousins very busy. Meanwhile Matthew took refuge in the quiet stable.

"How's the king of the stable?" teased Rebecca as she set a stool beside Jasmine.

"I'm not a king," growled Matthew.

"Well, pay attention," warned Rebecca as she placed a pail beneath the cow. "The king of the stable must also do the milking."

But Matthew didn't want to pay attention. And he was tired of being king of the stable. So he went outside and perched on a wooden crate and watched as people moved up and down the busy street. The bustling crowds reminded him of Jerusalem, and suddenly he missed his father and home more than ever.

Matthew looked on with misty eyes as more travelers approached his uncle's inn—a man and woman this time. Matthew could have told them the inn was full, but instead he watched in silence.

Matthew looked at the woman as she waited with the donkey. Her expression was weary and her brow creased in pain. Then suddenly she looked over at Matthew and smiled. And with that smile, the woman's tired face was transformed into a beautiful sweetness that reminded Matthew of his own dear mother. Matthew smiled back, then walked out to the street and patted the shaggy donkey.

"Have you been on the road for long?" asked Matthew.

"Yes, several days," she answered.

"I just arrived from Jerusalem today," said Matthew. "It was a long trip too."

The woman nodded. "Are you traveling with your family?"

Matthew shook his head sadly. "No, I'm alone. I had to leave my father behind."

The woman reached out and touched his shoulder. "I understand," she said. Then her face twisted in pain, and she hunched down against the donkey's neck.

"Are you all right?" asked Matthew.

"I will be soon. If only we can find a place to rest."

"Can I get you a drink of water?" offered Matthew.

"That would be nice," said the woman.

When Matthew returned with water, he overheard his uncle speaking to the man. "Sorry, son, my inn's been full since mid-morning. I think every inn in Bethlehem is full." Uncle Isaac shook his head and closed the door. Matthew handed the cup of water to the woman and watched as the man came back over.

"There's no room," said the man. "The innkeeper thinks all the inns are full."

The woman sighed. "What will we do? The baby is coming soon."

Matthew's eyes grew wide. "You—you're having a baby?"

"Yes," she answered with a faint smile, "a very important baby."

Matthew thought for a moment. "Please," he said, "don't leave. I have an idea!"

Matthew ran back into the inn and found his uncle, then told him the idea.

"It sounds like a good plan, Matthew," said Uncle Isaac. "But we're all very busy. Can you take care of the guests yourself?"

"Yes, Uncle Isaac," said Matthew. "I'll take care of everything!"

"So, the king of the stable is having guests now?" teased Rebecca.

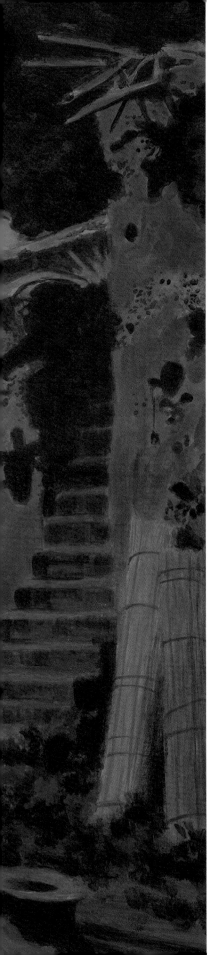

Matthew raced back out the door. "We have a place for you to stay!" he announced breathlessly. "It's all taken care of."

"Thank you," said the man as he clasped Matthew's hand. "We appreciate it. By the way, my name's Joseph, and this is my wife, Mary."

"I'm Matthew. I don't actually live here; it's my uncle's inn. But I'm trying to help." Matthew led the couple back to where the stable was situated behind the inn. Suddenly he felt worried. What would these nice people think about staying in a *stable*?

"I probably should explain that this isn't a *real* room," said Matthew. "You may not even like it. You see, I'm caring for my uncle's animals, and there's this empty stall. And well, it's clean and dry; and I'll put out fresh straw; and I'll get anything you need . . ."

"It sounds perfect," said Mary.

While Joseph unloaded the donkey, Matthew went to work spreading a fragrant carpet of straw over the hard-packed dirt floor. "I'll make a deep pile for a bed," he said as he heaped several forkfuls into the coziest corner of the vacant stall. "Then we can place blankets on top."

Mary looked around the stall, then smiled. "This was a good idea, Matthew. It's much more peaceful than a busy inn."

"I'm glad you like it," said Matthew with relief. "Believe me, I know it's not much. I'm used to living in my father's big, fine house with lots of servants. But I like it out here. It's quiet, and the animals are pleasant."

"It must be hard being away from your father," said Mary.

"It is. But my aunt and uncle are kind. And my cousins..." Matthew paused as he spread a blanket across the bed of straw, "... well, my cousins like to tease me."

"Tease you?" said Mary.

"Yes, they call me *king of the stable*."

"I see," said Mary with a knowing smile.

Thanks for your help—" Mary's words were cut short and she bent over, wrapping her arms around her middle and wincing in pain.

"Are you all right?" asked Matthew.

"She will be," said Joseph. "God is taking care of her. But we can use your help too." Joseph then told Matthew what they needed for the night.

It took a while, but finally Matthew gathered the provisions.

"Where did you get those blankets, Matthew?" asked Sarah.

"Don't worry, they're from my bed," said Matthew. "They're for my guests."

"*Your* guests?" said Sarah with raised brows. "The king of the stable has guests?"

"Yes, Uncle Isaac said it was all right."

"Where are you taking that jug of water?" asked Rachel.

"To my guests," answered Matthew proudly.

After several trips, Matthew delivered everything Mary and Joseph needed to spend the night in the stable. And, although he was curious, he knew it was time to leave them alone for the birth of their baby.

Matthew felt too excited to sleep. Instead, he sat outside and watched as a dazzling star lit the sky. It felt like something big was about to happen, and he didn't want to miss it. No, this was definitely not a night for sleeping.

Then he heard it—a sound that split the night! Loud cries of a newborn baby taking its first breaths drifted from the stable. Matthew waited and listened. Then finally, he crept over to the stable and peered in.

"Can I get you anything?" he said meekly.

Mary called, "Come in, Matthew. Come in and meet God's very own Son."

Matthew stared at the tiny baby nestled in a manger lined with hay. *"God's Son?"*

"That's right," said Mary. "His name is Jesus. He is the Son of God."

Matthew looked around the shabby stable. "But why would God allow His Son to be born in a place like this? Shouldn't God's Son be born in a fine palace?"

"Sometimes we can't understand why God works as He does," said Mary with a smile. "We just have to trust Him."

Matthew went back outside and considered Mary's odd words. *God's own Son?* He blinked up at the brilliant star and wondered. *Was it possible that the babe born in Uncle Isaac's stable tonight, the child who slept in a manger used for feeding livestock—could He possibly be the Son of God?*

Suddenly, Matthew was startled by happy voices. "Where is He?" they called out.

Matthew looked up to see a group of shepherds pouring into the yard behind his uncle's inn. "Where is *who*?" he asked.

"The Savior!" declared an elderly shepherd. "Angels woke us up tonight. They said we would find the Savior lying in a manger. Where is the Son of God?"

Matthew's jaw dropped as he stared at the shepherds. With a trembling finger he pointed toward Uncle Isaac's little stable. "In there," he stammered, "in the stable."

Matthew followed the shepherds into the stall and stared as, one by one, they fell to their knees and worshiped the sleeping baby.

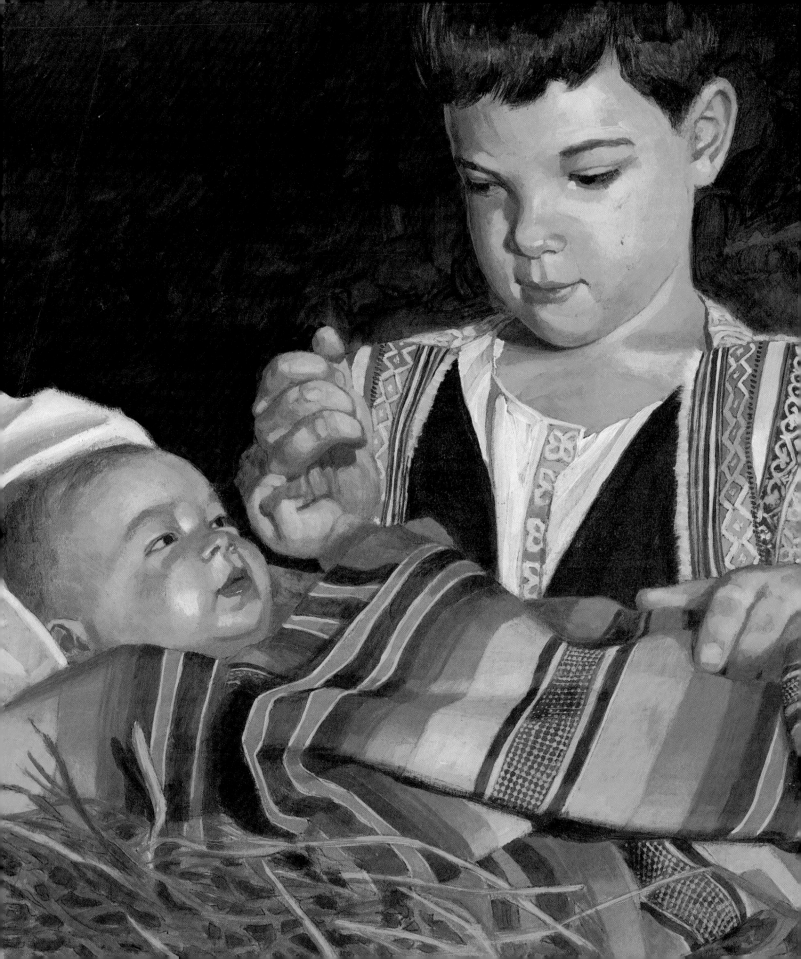

Matthew watched the shepherds bowing down . . . he glanced at the star gleaming brightly above . . . then he looked at the baby sleeping sweetly in the manger.

And suddenly Matthew knew. In his own heart he knew, without a shadow of doubt, that it was true! And Matthew, like the shepherds, fell to his knees and worshiped the tiny babe— the Son of God—the King of kings!

The next day Matthew gazed into Jesus' eyes. "You must know how I feel, Jesus," he said quietly. "I was sad to leave my father's house and come to a strange place. But when I think of how You left Your Father's house in heaven to come down to earth—" Matthew shook his head in wonder. "That must've been awfully hard."

Mary smiled at Matthew. "I see you and Jesus have something in common."

"Yes, but I'm only the king of the stable," said Matthew. "Jesus is the King of all kings."

"That's true," said Mary.

"And I will always serve Him," promised Matthew.

And he did.